S

MERCY
WITH
POPE FRANCIS

by
Amette Ley

*All booklets are published thanks to the
generous support of the members of the
Catholic Truth Society*

CATHOLIC TRUTH SOCIETY
PUBLISHERS TO THE HOLY SEE

CONTENTS

All rights reserved. First published 2016 by The Incorporated Catholic Truth Society, 40-46 Harleyford Road London SE11 5AY Tel: 020 7640 0042 Fax: 020 7640 0046. © 2016 The Incorporated Catholic Truth Society.

ISBN 978 1 78469 098 4

WALK WITH JESUS IN THE JUBILEE
YEAR OF MERCY

This Jubilee Year is an opportunity to live more intensely in the light of God's love, to celebrate and experience his everlasting mercy. The Church, through the authority and power of the Holy Spirit, has constantly proclaimed the mercy of God, in her Tradition and doctrines, in her liturgy and prayers. Pope Francis reminds us also of the wealth of Sacred Scripture appropriate for meditation to help us rediscover the merciful face of the Father:

> We can repeat the words of the prophet Micah and make them our own: You, O Lord, are a God who takes away iniquity and pardons sin, who does not hold your anger forever, but are pleased to show mercy. You, Lord, will return to us and have pity on your people. You will trample down our sins and toss them into the depths of the sea.[1]

With these words, Pope Francis invites us to walk with Jesus in this Jubilee Year 2015-2016 with renewed appreciation and thanksgiving for the mercy of God. Sometimes, the Holy Father reminds us, "…we are called to gaze even more attentively on mercy so that we may become a more effective sign of the Father's action in our lives."[2]

The Stations of the Cross are a traditional private devotion that evolved initially to help Christians meditate on the sufferings of Jesus as he was led to the cross. At first, many Christians were able to walk the very streets through which Jesus passed, even to Calvary. However, with the passage of time, the spread of the faith to distant lands and unrest in the Holy Land, this became impractical for most; then as now, the journey to the Holy Land was expensive and often dangerous. As a result, those who wished to accompany Jesus in this way set up 'stations' in the churches so that they could do so in the safety of their own parishes.

The devotion does not have set prayers in the way the liturgy does, though there are some well-known prayers, which have been included here. There have been many variations on both prayers and meditations, but for this Holy Year of Mercy we attempt to view the sufferings of Jesus as he was tried, tortured and crucified specifically through the lens of the mercy of God as expressed in the teachings of Pope Francis. At every station, in addition to a scriptural text and traditional prayers, there is a short extract from the writings of Pope Francis, each expressing some aspect of the mercy of God.

The Holy Father never makes a false opposition between justice and mercy. In speaking of the relationship between justice and mercy he affirms:

These are not two contradictory realities, but two dimensions of a single reality that unfolds progressively until it culminates in the fullness of love. Justice is a fundamental concept for civil society, which is meant to be governed by the rule of law. Justice is also understood as that which is rightly due to each individual. In the Bible, there are many references to divine justice and to God as 'judge'. In these passages, justice is understood as the full observance of the Law and the behaviour of every good Israelite in conformity with God's commandments. Such a vision, however, has not infrequently led to legalism by distorting the original meaning of justice and obscuring its profound value. To overcome this legalistic perspective, we need to recall that in Sacred Scripture, justice is conceived essentially as the faithful abandonment of oneself to God's will.[3]

Therefore, in considering the mercy of God, we are not rejecting justice, but responding to our loving Father in heaven who calls us into his own Trinitarian life. "Mercy is not opposed to justice but rather expresses God's way of reaching out to the sinner, offering him a new chance to look at himself, convert, and believe."[4]

The Holy Father also teaches us that it is not enough that we should ourselves ask for and receive mercy from God, but that we in turn must be merciful to others. He reminds us of the parable Our Lord told in answer to Peter's question about how many times we should forgive others. (*Mt* 18:22)

Jesus affirms that mercy is not only an action of the Father, it becomes a criterion for ascertaining who his true children are. In short, we are called to show mercy because mercy has first been shown to us. Pardoning offences becomes the clearest expression of merciful love, and for us Christians it is an imperative from which we cannot excuse ourselves.[5]

"Blessed are the merciful, for they shall obtain mercy" (*Mt* 5:7). This, the Holy Father tells us, is the beatitude to which we should particularly aspire in this Holy Year. The poet Alexander Pope expresses this aspiration beautifully:

> Teach me to feel another's woe,
> To hide the fault I see;
> That mercy I to others show,
> That mercy show to me.[6]

As so many have done before him, the Holy Father invites us to turn to our Blessed Mother, given to us at the foot of the cross, and ask her to pray with us and for us:

> Together let us pray to the Virgin Mary that she helps us...to walk in faith and charity, ever trusting in the Lord's mercy; he always awaits us, loves us, has pardoned us with his Blood and pardons us every time we go to him to ask his forgiveness. Let us trust in his mercy![7]

May the sweetness of her countenance watch over us in this Holy Year, so that all of us may rediscover the joy of God's tenderness.[8]

PRAYER

Lord Jesus Christ,
you have taught us to be merciful like
    the heavenly Father,
and have told us that whoever sees you sees him.
Show us your face and we will be saved.
Your loving gaze freed Zacchaeus and Matthew
    from being enslaved by money;
the adulteress and Magdalene from seeking
    happiness only in created things;
made Peter weep after his betrayal,
and assured Paradise to the repentant thief.
Let us hear, as if addressed to each one of us,
    the words that you spoke to the Samaritan woman:
"If you knew the gift of God!"
We ask this through the intercession of Mary,
    Mother of Mercy,
you who live and reign with the Father and
    the Holy Spirit for ever and ever.
Amen.

I

THE FIRST STATION
JESUS IS CONDEMNED TO DEATH

V. (genuflecting) *We adore you, O Christ, and we bless you.*
R. *Because by your Holy Cross you have redeemed the world.*

Scripture

Pilate…brought Jesus out and sat down on the judgement seat at a place called The Pavement, and in Hebrew, Gabbatha… He said to the Jews, "Behold your King!" They cried out, "Away with him, away with him, crucify him!" Pilate said to them, "Shall I crucify your King?" The chief priests answered, "We have no king but Caesar." Then he handed him over to them to be crucified. (*Jn* 19:13-16)

Pope Francis

"I think we too are the people who, on the one hand, want to listen to Jesus, but on the other hand, at times, like to find a stick to beat others with, to condemn others. And Jesus has this message for us: mercy. I think…that this is the Lord's most powerful message: mercy."[9]

PRAYER
I love you, Jesus, my love above all things.
I repent with my whole heart for having offended you.
Never permit me to separate myself from you again.
Grant that I may love you always, and then do with me what you will.

II

THE SECOND STATION
JESUS ACCEPTS THE CROSS

V. (genuflecting) *We adore you, O Christ, and we bless you.*
R. *Because by your Holy Cross you have redeemed the world.*

Scripture

So they took Jesus, and he went out, bearing his own cross, to the place called the place of a skull, which is called in Hebrew Golgotha. (*Jn* 19:17)

Pope Francis

"The cross is not an ornament that we must always put in the churches…It is not a symbol that distinguishes us from others. The cross is mystery, the mystery of God who humbles himself, he becomes 'nothing'… Christianity is a person, a person raised on the cross, a person who annihilated himself to save us. It is impossible for us to free ourselves from sin on our own. You cannot understand Christianity without understanding this profound humiliation of the Son of God who humbled himself and became a servant unto death, even death on a cross, in order to serve us."[10]

PRAYER
I love you, Jesus, my love above all things.
I repent with my whole heart for having offended you.
Never permit me to separate myself from you again.
Grant that I may love you always, and then do with me what you will.

III

THE THIRD STATION
JESUS FALLS THE FIRST TIME

V. (genuflecting) *We adore you, O Christ, and we bless you.*
R. *Because by your Holy Cross you have redeemed the world.*

Scripture

Now the men who were holding Jesus mocked him and beat him; they also blindfolded him and asked him, "Prophesy! Who is it that struck you?" And they spoke many other words against him, reviling him. (*Lk* 22:63)

Pope Francis

"God's patience has to call forth in us the courage to return to him, however many mistakes and sins there may be in our life… It is there, in the wounds of Jesus, that we are truly secure; there we encounter the boundless love of his heart."[11]

PRAYER
I love you, Jesus, my love above all things.
I repent with my whole heart for having offended you.
Never permit me to separate myself from you again.
Grant that I may love you always, and then do with me what you will.

IV

THE FOURTH STATION
JESUS MEETS HIS BLESSED MOTHER

V. (genuflecting) *We adore you, O Christ, and we bless you.*
R. *Because by your Holy Cross you have redeemed the world.*

Scripture

He who is mighty has done great things for me, and holy is his name. And his mercy is on those who fear him from generation to generation. (*Lk* 1:49-50)

Pope Francis

"[Mary] treasured divine mercy in her heart in perfect harmony with her Son Jesus. Her hymn of praise, sung at the threshold of the home of Elizabeth, was dedicated to the mercy of God which extends from 'generation to generation' (*Lk* 1:50). We too were included in those prophetic words of the Virgin Mary."[12]

PRAYER
I love you, Jesus, my love above all things.
I repent with my whole heart for having offended you.
Never permit me to separate myself from you again.
Grant that I may love you always, and then do with me what you will.

V

THE FIFTH STATION
THE CROSS IS LAID UPON
SIMON OF CYRENE

V. (genuflecting) *We adore you, O Christ, and we bless you.*
R. *Because by your Holy Cross you have redeemed the world.*

Scripture

As they led him away, they seized one Simon of Cyrene, who was coming in from the country, and laid on him the cross, to carry it behind Jesus. (*Lk* 23:26)

Pope Francis

"To be a Christian means to be a 'Cyrene'. Having the faith consists in this: you belong to Jesus if you bear the weight of the cross with him. Otherwise you are going along a path that seems 'good' - but is not 'true'. Step by step [Jesus] prepares us so that we can understand better. He prepares us to accompany him with our crosses, along his path to Redemption. He prepares us to be 'Cyrenes' to help him bear the cross."[13]

PRAYER
I love you, Jesus, my love above all things.
I repent with my whole heart for having offended you.
Never permit me to separate myself from you again.
Grant that I may love you always, and then do with me
what you will.

VI

THE SIXTH STATION
VERONICA WIPES THE FACE OF JESUS

V. (genuflecting) *We adore you, O Christ, and we bless you.*
R. *Because by your Holy Cross you have redeemed the world.*

Scripture

Your face, Lord, do I seek. Do not hide your face from me. Do not turn your servant away in anger, you who have been my help. Do not cast me off, do not forsake me, O God of my salvation! (*Ps* 27:8-9)

Pope Francis

"God's face is the face of a merciful father who is always patient. Have you thought about God's patience, the patience he has with each one of us? That is his mercy. He always has patience, patience with us, he understands us, he waits for us, he does not tire of forgiving us if we are able to return to him with a contrite heart. 'Great is God's mercy,' says the Psalm."[14]

PRAYER

I love you, Jesus, my love above all things.
I repent with my whole heart for having offended you.
Never permit me to separate myself from you again.
Grant that I may love you always, and then do with me what you will.

VII

THE SEVENTH STATION
JESUS FALLS THE SECOND TIME

V. (genuflecting) *We adore you, O Christ, and we bless you.*
R. *Because by your Holy Cross you have redeemed the world.*

Scripture

Surely he has borne our griefs and carried our sorrows; yet we esteemed him stricken, smitten by God, and afflicted. But he was wounded for our transgressions, he was bruised for our iniquities; upon him was the chastisement that made us whole, and with his stripes we are healed. (*Is* 53:4-5)

Pope Francis

"If a Christian wants to move forward on the road of Christian life he must fall, just as Jesus fell. It is the way of humility, yes, it also means he must take humiliation upon himself just as Jesus did."[15]

PRAYER
I love you, Jesus, my love above all things.
I repent with my whole heart for having offended you.
Never permit me to separate myself from you again.
Grant that I may love you always, and then do with me what you will.

VIII

THE EIGHTH STATION
THE WOMEN OF JERUSALEM
MOURN FOR JESUS

V. (genuflecting) *We adore you, O Christ, and we bless you.*
R. *Because by your Holy Cross you have redeemed the world.*

Scripture

There followed him a great multitude of the people, and of women who bewailed and lamented him. But Jesus turning to them said, "Daughters of Jerusalem, do not weep for me, but weep for yourselves and for your children." (*Lk* 23:27-28)

Pope Francis

"With our eyes fixed on Jesus and his merciful gaze, we experience the love of the Most Holy Trinity... 'God is love' (*1 Jn* 4:8,16), John affirms for the first and only time in all of Holy Scripture. This love has now been made visible and tangible in Jesus's entire life. His person is nothing but love, a love given gratuitously. The relationships he forms with the people who approach him manifest something entirely unique and unrepeatable... Everything in him speaks of mercy."[16]

PRAYER
I love you, Jesus, my love above all things.
I repent with my whole heart for having offended you.
Never permit me to separate myself from you again.
Grant that I may love you always, and then do with me what you will.

IX

THE NINTH STATION
JESUS FALLS FOR THE THIRD TIME

V. (genuflecting) *We adore you, O Christ, and we bless you.*
R. *Because by your Holy Cross you have redeemed the world.*

Scripture

You, O Lord, are a God who takes away iniquity and pardons sin, who does not hold your anger forever, but are pleased to show mercy. You, Lord, will return to us and have pity on your people. (*Mi* 7:18-19)

Pope Francis

"The Church is commissioned to announce the mercy of God, the beating heart of the Gospel, which…must penetrate the heart and mind of every person… It is absolutely essential for the Church…that she herself live and testify to mercy. Her language and her gestures must transmit mercy, so as to touch the hearts of all people and inspire them once more to find the road that leads to the Father."[17]

PRAYER
I love you, Jesus, my love above all things.
I repent with my whole heart for having offended you.
Never permit me to separate myself from you again.
Grant that I may love you always, and then do with me
what you will.

X

THE TENTH STATION
JESUS IS STRIPPED OF HIS GARMENTS

V. (genuflecting) *We adore you, O Christ, and we bless you.*
R. *Because by your Holy Cross you have redeemed the world.*

Scripture

And when they came to a place called Golgotha (which means the place of a skull), they offered him wine to drink, mingled with gall, but when he tasted it, he would not drink it. And when they had crucified him, they divided his garments among them by casting lots. (*Mt* 27:33-35)

Pope Francis

"Christ, who told us to forgive one another 'seventy times seven' (*Mt* 18:22) has given us his example: he has forgiven us seventy times seven… No one can strip us of the dignity bestowed upon us by this boundless and unfailing love. With a tenderness which never disappoints, but is always capable of restoring our joy, he makes it possible for us to lift up our heads and to start anew."[18]

PRAYER
I love you, Jesus, my love above all things.
I repent with my whole heart for having offended you.
Never permit me to separate myself from you again.
Grant that I may love you always, and then do with me what you will.

XI

THE ELEVENTH STATION
JESUS IS NAILED TO THE CROSS

V. (genuflecting) *We adore you, O Christ, and we bless you.*
R. *Because by your Holy Cross you have redeemed the world.*

Scripture

And when they came to the place which is called The Skull, there they crucified him, and the criminals, one on the right and one on the left. And Jesus said, "Father, forgive them; for they know not what they do." (*Lk* 23:33-34)

Pope Francis

"Jesus Christ is the face of the Father's mercy. These words might well sum up the mystery of the Christian faith. Mercy has become living and visible in Jesus of Nazareth, reaching its culmination in him… Jesus of Nazareth, by his words, his actions, and his entire person reveals the mercy of God."[19]

PRAYER

I love you, Jesus, my love above all things.
I repent with my whole heart for having offended you.
Never permit me to separate myself from you again.
Grant that I may love you always, and then do with me what you will.

XII

THE TWELFTH STATION
JESUS DIES ON THE CROSS

V. (genuflecting) *We adore you, O Christ, and we bless you.*
R. *Because by your Holy Cross you have redeemed the world.*

Scripture

When Jesus saw his mother, and the disciple whom he loved standing near, he said to his mother, "Woman, behold, your son!" Then he said to the disciple, "Behold, your mother!" And from that hour the disciple took her to his own home. (*Jn* 19:26-27)

Pope Francis

"On the cross, when Jesus endured in his own flesh the dramatic encounter of the sin of the world and God's mercy, he could feel at his feet the consoling presence of his mother and his friend. At that crucial moment, before fully accomplishing the work which his Father had entrusted to him, Jesus said to Mary: 'Woman, here is your son'. Then he said to his beloved friend: 'Here is your mother' (*Jn* 19:26-27)… Jesus left us his mother to be our mother. Only after doing so did Jesus know that 'all was now finished.'"[20]

PRAYER
I love you, Jesus, my love above all things.
I repent with my whole heart for having offended you.
Never permit me to separate myself from you again.
Grant that I may love you always, and then do with me what you will.

XIII

THE THIRTEENTH STATION
JESUS IS TAKEN DOWN FROM THE CROSS

V. (genuflecting) *We adore you, O Christ, and we bless you.*
R. *Because by your Holy Cross you have redeemed the world.*

Scripture

After this Joseph of Arimathea…asked Pilate that he might take away the body of Jesus, and Pilate gave him leave. So he came and took away his body. Nicodemus also…came bringing a mixture of myrrh and aloes, about a hundred pounds' weight. They took the body of Jesus, and bound it in linen cloths with the spices. (*Jn* 19:38-40)

Pope Francis

"We need constantly to contemplate the mystery of mercy… Our salvation depends on it. Mercy: the word reveals the very mystery of the Most Holy Trinity. Mercy: the ultimate and supreme act by which God comes to meet us. Mercy: the fundamental law that dwells in the heart of every person… Mercy: the bridge that connects God and man."[21]

PRAYER
I love you, Jesus, my love above all things.
I repent with my whole heart for having offended you.
Never permit me to separate myself from you again.
Grant that I may love you always, and then do with me
what you will.

XIV

THE FOURTEENTH STATION
JESUS IS PLACED IN THE TOMB

V. (kneeling) *We adore you, O Christ, and we bless you.*
R. *Because by your Holy Cross you have redeemed the world.*

Scripture

Now in the place where he was crucified there was a garden, and in the garden a new tomb where no one had ever been laid. So because of the Jewish day of Preparation, as the tomb was close at hand, they laid Jesus there. (*Jn* 19:41-42)

Pope Francis

"God's mercy can make even the driest land become a garden, can restore life to dry bones... Let us be renewed by God's mercy, let us be loved by Jesus, let us enable the power of his love to transform our lives too; and let us become agents of this mercy, channels through which God can water the earth, protect all creation and make justice and peace flourish."[22]

PRAYER
I love you, Jesus, my love above all things.
I repent with my whole heart for having offended you.
Never permit me to separate myself from you again.
Grant that I may love you always, and then do with me what you will.

For the Holy Father's intentions
Our Father... Hail Mary... Glory be...

Closing Prayer

Lord Jesus Christ,
You are the visible face of the invisible Father,
of the God who manifests his power above all
    by forgiveness and mercy:
let the Church be your visible face in the world,
    its Lord risen and glorified.
You willed that your ministers would also be
    clothed in weakness
in order that they may feel compassion for those
    in ignorance and error:
let everyone who approaches them feel sought after,
    loved, and forgiven by God.

Send your Spirit and consecrate every one of us
    with its anointing,
so that the Jubilee of Mercy may be a year of grace
    from the Lord,
and your Church, with renewed enthusiasm,
    may bring good news to the poor,
proclaim liberty to captives and the oppressed,
    and restore sight to the blind.

We ask this of you, Lord Jesus,
through the intercession of Mary, Mother of Mercy;
you who live and reign with the Father and
    the Holy Spirit for ever and ever.
Amen.

PRAYERS FOR MERCY

Prayer for compassion

God of mercy and compassion,
Look with pity upon me,
Father, let me call Thee Father,
'Tis Thy child returns to Thee.

Jesus, Lord, I ask for mercy;
Let me not implore in vain;
All my sins, I now detest them,
Never will I sin again.

Hail Holy Queen

Hail, holy Queen, Mother of mercy, hail, our life, our sweetness and our hope. To thee do we cry, poor banished children of Eve: to thee do we send up our sighs, mourning and weeping in this vale of tears. Turn then, most gracious Advocate, thine eyes of mercy toward us, and after this our exile, show unto us the blessed fruit of thy womb, Jesus, O merciful, O loving, O sweet Virgin Mary! Amen.

Prayer to Our Lady of Mercy

Blessed Virgin Mary,
who can worthily repay you with praise
and thanks for having rescued a fallen world
by your generous consent!
Receive our gratitude,
and by your prayers obtain the pardon of our sins.
Take our prayers into the sanctuary of heaven
and enable them to make our peace with God.

Holy Mary, help the miserable,
strengthen the discouraged,
comfort the sorrowful,
pray for your people,
plead for the clergy,
intercede for all women consecrated to God.
May all who venerate you
feel now your help and protection.
Be ready to help us when we pray,
and bring back to us the answers to our prayers.
Make it your continual concern
to pray for the people of God,
for you were blessed by God
and were made worthy to bear the Redeemer
of the world,
who lives and reigns forever.
Amen.

(St Augustine of Hippo)

Prayers for mercy and strength

O God, who make known your almighty power
above all by pardoning and showing mercy,
bestow, we pray, your grace abundantly upon us,
and make those hastening to attain your promises
heirs to the treasures of heaven.
We make our prayer through our Lord Jesus Christ.

God, the strength of all those who put their trust in you
mercifully accept our prayers
and, because through the weakness of our mortal nature
we can do no good thing without you,
grant us the help of your grace,
that in the keeping of your commandments
we may please you both in will and deed;
through Jesus Christ our Lord.

O God, the protector of all who trust in you,
without whom nothing is strong, nothing is holy:
increase and multiply upon us your mercy;
that with you as our ruler and guide,
we may so pass through things temporal
that we finally lose not our hold on things eternal;
grant this heavenly Father,
for Jesus Christ's sake, our Lord.

About the artist

Arturo Vonn Hartung is an artist of Catholic Sacred Art, primarily a painter and wood sculptor, although he has also done major works in mosaic, ceramic sculpture, portraits and serigraphs. His inspirations include all kind of Catholic art, especially Michelangelo. Originally from Connecticut, USA, he has lived in Mexico and, since 1984, has lived in Puerto Rico, where he painted Stations of the Cross for Santa Rosa de Lima Church in Guaynabo (Barrio Amelia), Puerto Rico. The artist conceived them with the community in mind and they include much of the spiritual and cultural qualities of Puerto Rico. Each Station measures 4-ft by 8-ft, painted in acrylic and gilded in copper and gold.

www.avonnhartung.com

Endnotes

[1] Bull of Indiction of the Extraordinary Jubilee of Mercy, *Misericordiae Vultus*, 11th April 2015, 17.
[2] *Misericordiae Vultus* 3.
[3] *Misericordiae Vultus* 20.
[4] *Misericordiae Vultus* 21.
[5] *Misericordiae Vultus* 9.
[6] Alexander Pope, 'The Universal Prayer'.
[7] Regina Caeli, Divine Mercy Sunday, 7th April 2013.
[8] *Misericordiae Vultus* 24.
[9] Homily on 17th March 2013.
[10] Homily, Mass at Santa Marta, 8th April 2014.
[11] Homily on Divine Mercy Sunday, 7th April 2014.
[12] *Misericordiae Vultus* 24.
[13] Mass at Santa Marta, 26th September 2014.
[14] Angelus, 17th March 2013.
[15] Mass at Santa Marta, 14th September 2015.
[16] *Misericordiae Vultus* 8.
[17] *Misericordiae Vultus* 12.
[18] *Evangelii Gaudium* 3.
[19] *Misericordiae Vultus* 1.
[20] *Evangelii Gaudium* 285.
[21] *Misericordiae Vultus* 2.
[22] Easter *Urbi et Orbi* message, 31st March 2013.